A MEDIEVAL CHRISTMAS

Christmas Blessings for
Mom and Dad 2003
with love, mike

✠

The words of Scripture are taken from the
Revised Standard Version, Catholic Edition, second edition, 2003.
They are from the Gospels of St. Matthew and St. Luke.

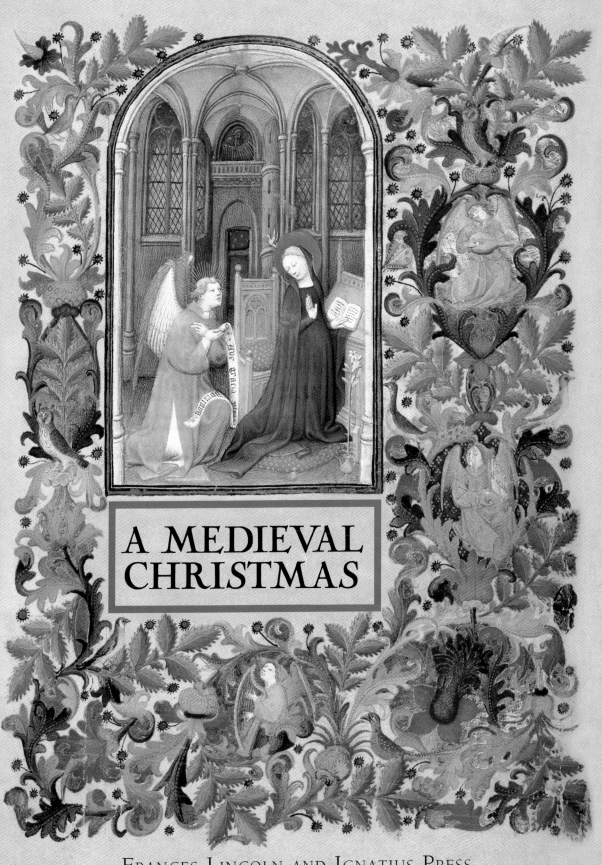

A MEDIEVAL CHRISTMAS

FRANCES LINCOLN AND IGNATIUS PRESS
in association with
THE BRITISH LIBRARY

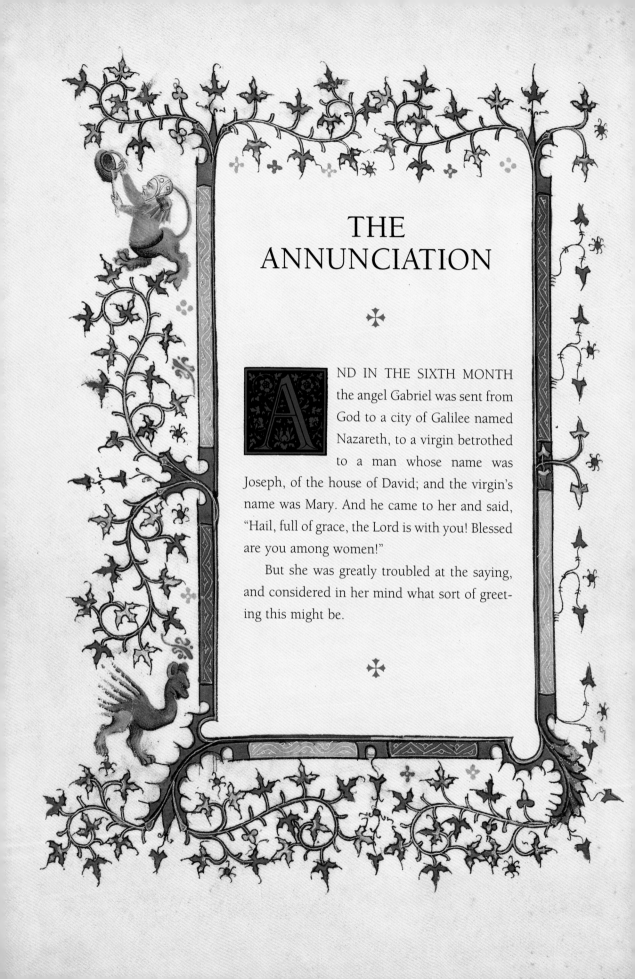

THE ANNUNCIATION

✠

AND IN THE SIXTH MONTH the angel Gabriel was sent from God to a city of Galilee named Nazareth, to a virgin betrothed to a man whose name was Joseph, of the house of David; and the virgin's name was Mary. And he came to her and said, "Hail, full of grace, the Lord is with you! Blessed are you among women!"

But she was greatly troubled at the saying, and considered in her mind what sort of greeting this might be.

✠

THE ANNUNCIATION

AND THE ANGEL SAID TO HER, "Do not be afraid, Mary, for you have found favor with God. And behold, you will conceive in your womb and bear a son, and you shall call his name Jesus. He will be great, and will be called the Son of the Most High; and the Lord God will give to him the throne of his father David, and he will reign over the house of Jacob for ever; and of his kingdom there will be no end."

And Mary said to the angel, "How will this be, since I have no husband?" And the angel said to her, "The Holy Spirit will come upon you, and the power of the Most High will overshadow you; therefore the child to be born will be called holy, the Son of God. And behold, your kinswoman Elizabeth in her old age has also conceived a son; and this is the sixth month with her who was called barren. For with God nothing will be impossible." And Mary said, "Behold, I am the handmaid of the Lord; let it be to me according to your word." And the angel departed from her.

THE VISITATION

✠

AND IN THOSE DAYS MARY AROSE and went with haste into the hill country, to a city of Judah, and she entered the house of Zechariah and greeted Elizabeth. And when Elizabeth heard the greeting of Mary, the child leaped in her womb; and Elizabeth was filled with the Holy Spirit and she exclaimed with a loud cry, "Blessed are you among women, and blessed is the fruit of your womb! And why is this granted me, that the mother of my Lord should come to me? For behold, when the voice of your greeting came to my ears, the child in my womb leaped for joy. And blessed is she who believed that there would be a fulfilment of what was spoken to her from the Lord."

And Mary remained with her about three months, and returned to her home.

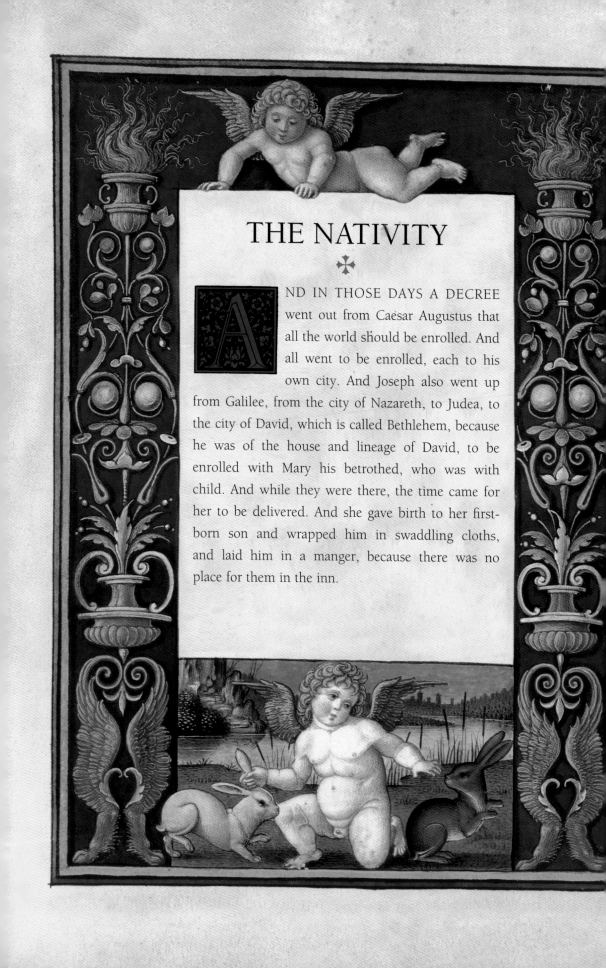

THE NATIVITY

✤

AND IN THOSE DAYS A DECREE went out from Caesar Augustus that all the world should be enrolled. And all went to be enrolled, each to his own city. And Joseph also went up from Galilee, from the city of Nazareth, to Judea, to the city of David, which is called Bethlehem, because he was of the house and lineage of David, to be enrolled with Mary his betrothed, who was with child. And while they were there, the time came for her to be delivered. And she gave birth to her first-born son and wrapped him in swaddling cloths, and laid him in a manger, because there was no place for them in the inn.

ens Adcnnam.
madutouum
meum intende.
Domine ad admiandū

ANNUNCIATION TO THE SHEPHERDS

AND IN THAT REGION there were shepherds out in the field, keeping watch over their flock by night. And an angel of the Lord appeared to them, and the glory of the Lord shone around them, and they were filled with fear. And the angel said to them, "Be not afraid; for behold, I bring you good news of a great joy which will come to all the people; for to you is born this day in the city of David a Savior, who is Christ the Lord."

And they went with haste, and found Mary and Joseph, and the baby lying in a manger.

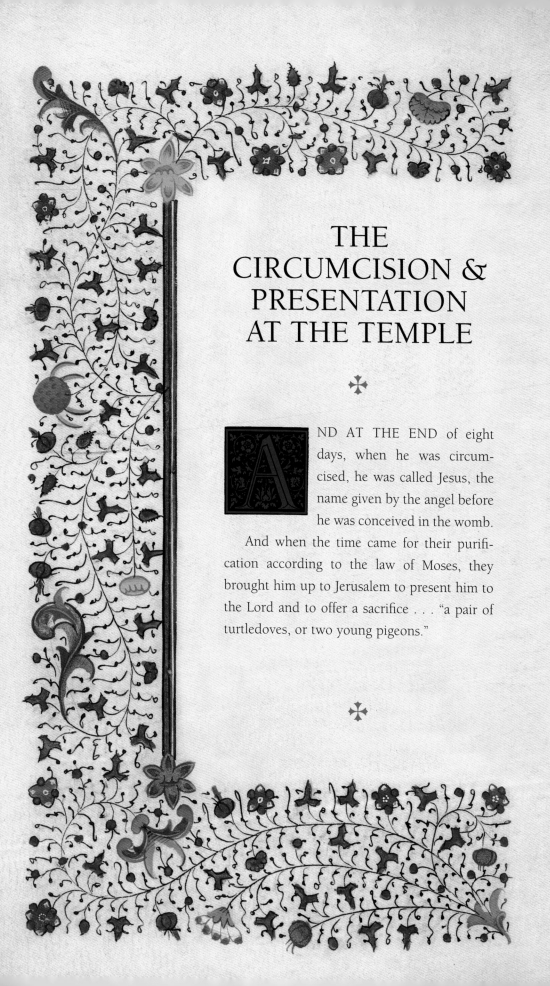

THE CIRCUMCISION & PRESENTATION AT THE TEMPLE

✠

AND AT THE END of eight days, when he was circumcised, he was called Jesus, the name given by the angel before he was conceived in the womb.

And when the time came for their purification according to the law of Moses, they brought him up to Jerusalem to present him to the Lord and to offer a sacrifice . . . "a pair of turtledoves, or two young pigeons."

✠

THE EPIPHANY

✠

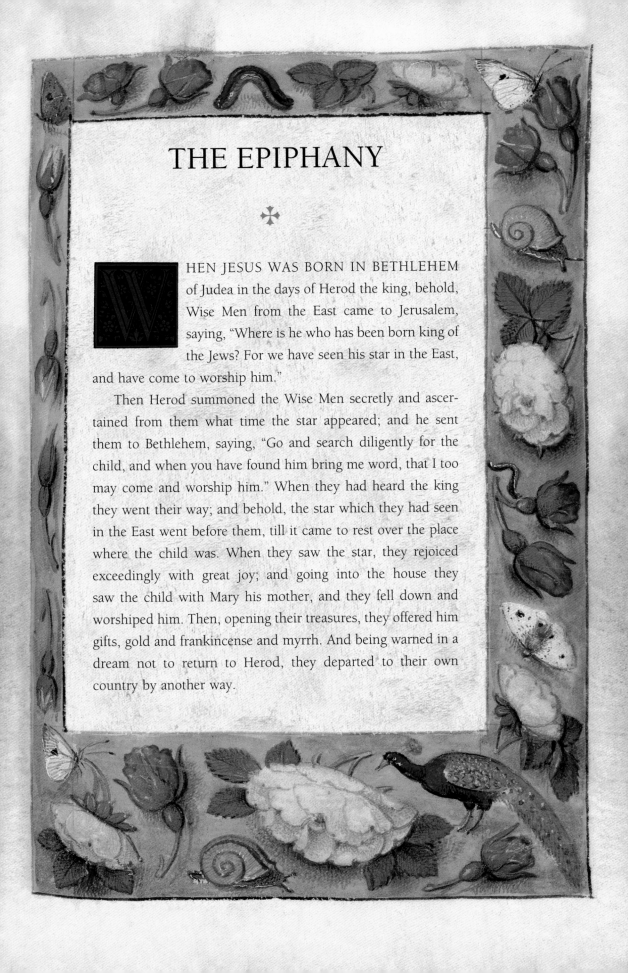

WHEN JESUS WAS BORN IN BETHLEHEM of Judea in the days of Herod the king, behold, Wise Men from the East came to Jerusalem, saying, "Where is he who has been born king of the Jews? For we have seen his star in the East, and have come to worship him."

Then Herod summoned the Wise Men secretly and ascertained from them what time the star appeared; and he sent them to Bethlehem, saying, "Go and search diligently for the child, and when you have found him bring me word, that I too may come and worship him." When they had heard the king they went their way; and behold, the star which they had seen in the East went before them, till it came to rest over the place where the child was. When they saw the star, they rejoiced exceedingly with great joy; and going into the house they saw the child with Mary his mother, and they fell down and worshiped him. Then, opening their treasures, they offered him gifts, gold and frankincense and myrrh. And being warned in a dream not to return to Herod, they departed to their own country by another way.

THE FLIGHT
TO EGYPT

✠

WHEN THEY HAD DEPARTED, behold, an angel of the Lord appeared to Joseph in a dream and said, "Rise, take the child and his mother, and flee to Egypt, and remain there till I tell you; for Herod is about to search for the child, to destroy him." And he rose and took the child and his mother by night, and departed to Egypt, and remained there until the death of Herod. This was to fulfil what the Lord had spoken by the prophet, "Out of Egypt have I called my son."

THE HOLY FAMILY

✤

WHEN HEROD DIED, behold, an angel of the Lord appeared in a dream to Joseph in Egypt, saying, "Rise, take the child and his mother, and go to the land of Israel, for those who sought the child's life are dead." And he rose and took the child and his mother, and went to the land of Israel. But when he heard that Archelaus reigned over Judea in place of his father Herod, he was afraid to go there, and being warned in a dream he withdrew to the district of Galilee. And he went and dwelt in a city called Nazareth, that what was spoken by the prophets might be fulfilled. "He shall be called a Nazarene."

(LEFT) *Front cover*

The Bedford Hours. BL Additional MS
18850 f.65. Paris, about 1423.
260 x 180 mm

THE BEDFORD HOURS, one of the
grandest illuminated manuscripts
ever produced, was originally owned by
John of Lancaster, Duke of Bedford and his
wife Anne of Burgundy, married in 1423.
On Christmas Eve 1430, the Duchess, with
her husband's approval, offered the Hours
as a gift to their nephew, nine year old
Henry VI, who was staying with them at
Rouen before his French coronation. The
marginal decoration of the manuscript is
unusually rich and original, comprising
over a thousand small, circular miniatures.

(RIGHT) *Page 7 (title page)*

Hours of Etienne Chevalier.
BL Additional MS 16997 f.21.
France, early 15th century.
160 x 115 mm

THIS EXQUISITE SMALL Book of Hours,
regarded as one of the artist's finest
works, was illuminated in the first quarter
of the 15th century by the Boucicaut
Master, a leading Parisian book painter of
the day. He is named in honour of his
principal patron, the Maréchal de
Boucicaut, who was taken prisoner at the
Battle of Agincourt and died in England
in 1421.

(LEFT) *Pages 8 - 9*

THE ANNUNCIATION

BL Additional MS 30899 f.1.
Paris, early 15th century.
200 x 140 mm

ONE OF SIX detached leaves from a
Book of Hours, typical of the best
contemporary Parisian illumination. The
delicate marginal decoration, along with
singing angels, includes a pair of putti
fencing with windmills. The arms of an
early owner have been painted out in the
lower margin.

THE ANNUNCIATION

The Hastings Hours. BL Additional MS
54782 f.73. Flemish, about 1480.
165 x 120 mm

Tᴴɪꜱ ᴍᴀɴᴜꜱᴄʀɪᴘᴛ was made for William,
Lord Hastings, a close friend of King
Edward IV. Hastings was beheaded in 1483
on the orders of the Duke of Gloucester,
afterwards King Richard III. Its delicate,
beautiful miniatures, surrounded by
superb illusionistic floral borders, place it
among the very finest of the manuscripts
produced in Flanders by the founders of
the Ghent/Bruges School, one of the last
great styles of illumination. Lord Hastings'
arms appear in the margin of the recto.

(ABOVE) *Page 12*

THE VISITATION

BL Egerton MS 1070 f.29v. French,
early 15th century.
220 x 160 mm

Tᴴɪꜱ ᴍᴀɴᴜꜱᴄʀɪᴘᴛ was painted by one of
the leading Parisian illuminators of the
early 15th century. It later belonged to
René of Anjou, titular king of Naples and
Jerusalem, who died in 1480. His daughter
Margaret was married to King Henry VI of
England. The recto (page 13) contains an
image which has been replaced by text for
the purposes of this book.

(ABOVE) *Pages 14 – 15*

THE NATIVITY

The Sforza Hours. BL Additional MS 34294 f.82v.
Italian, about 1490, with Flemish additions
made in 1519.
130 x 95 mm

Tᴴᴇ ᴏʀɪɢɪɴᴀʟ ᴏᴡɴᴇʀ of the manuscript, illuminated
by the Milanese court painter Pietro Birago, was
Bona of Savoy (D 1503), the wife of Galeazzo Maria
Sforza, Duke of Milan. Unfinished at the time of her
death, the manuscript eventually passed into the hands
of Margaret of Austria who paid the Flemish miniaturist,
Gerard Horenbout, to provide the 16 miniatures,
including this Nativity, needed to complete the work
containing 64 miniatures in total. Horenbout took great
pains to copy the format and range of colouring which he
found in the book's Italian miniatures, but his landscapes
and the faces of his characters are typically Flemish.

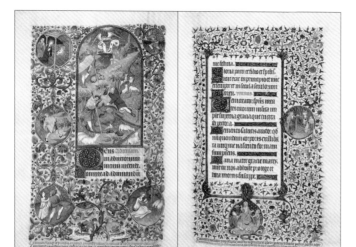

(Left) *Pages 16 – 17*

The Annunciation to the Shepherds

The Bedford Hours. BL Additional MS
18850 f.70v. Paris, about 1423.
260 x 180 mm
(*See entry for cover image*)

Each of the main miniatures of the manuscript is accompanied by an elaborate set of marginal roundels. The marginal roundels decorating the text pages cover the whole of the New Testament, each episode accompanied either by its Old Testament prefiguration, or by some form of pictorial commentary. The reader's understanding is aided by explanatory 'subtitles' written at the bottom; on the text pages, they are written in blue and gold and on each main miniature page, in blue and red.

(Right) *Pages 18 – 19*

The Presentation in the Temple

Additional MS 31834 f.66.
Paris, second quarter of the 15th century.
245 x 175 mm

In this version of the Presentation, the Jewish priest is shown garbed as a Christian bishop. The manuscript is one of a number bequeathed to the national collection in 1881 by William Burges, the Victorian architect and designer, whose own work was heavily influenced by medieval models.

(Left) *Pages 20 – 21*

The Epiphany

Egerton MS 2125 f.182v.
Flemish, early 16th century.
155 x 100 mm

This elegant little book, containing 22 miniatures and borders of flowers, insects and jewels, was made in the workshop of the celebrated Flemish illuminator Simon Bening, apparently for the personal use of the abbess of Messines, near Ypres in West Flanders.

(RIGHT) *Pages 22 – 23 and back cover*
(detail)

THE FLIGHT TO EGYPT

Additional MS 25695 f.114.
Paris, about 1470.
190 x 135 mm

THE STORY OF Joseph's dream is told on a scroll wound around the tree trunks that enclose the main miniature. Inside a bejewelled frame the Holy Family crosses the foreground. Behind them a farmer is interrogated by Herod's soldiers. The margins of the folio are peopled with figures depicting the story of the Massacre of the Innocents.

(LEFT) *Pages 24 – 25*

THE HOLY FAMILY

Additional MS 18193 f.48v.
Spanish, second half of the 15th century.
195 x 135 mm

A SPECIAL MASS in honour of the Virgin is frequently found in Books of Hours. In this manuscript it begins with an illustration of the Holy Family in St Joseph's carpenter's shop. An array of tools hangs from the wall at the back of the picture, most of them very little different from those in use today. The Virgin is at work on some embroidery, her materials supported on a cushion and a work-basket at her side. The Child has toys and a bird in a cage. The entire scene could represent an episode in the contemporary everyday life.

A Medieval Christmas © 1996 Frances Lincoln Limited

Revised Standard Version of the Holy Bible, the Old Testament © 1952, Catholic edition © 1966, the Apocrypha © 1957, 1966, the New Testament © 1946, Catholic edition © 1965, Second Catholic edition © 2003, by the Division of Christian Education of the National Council of the Churches of Christ in the United States of America.

First published in Great Britain in 1996 by
Frances Lincoln Limited, 4 Torriano Mews, Torriano Avenue, London NW5 2RZ

ISBN 0–89870–991–1

Design by David Fordham
Printed in China